CHRISTM

CW01424695

THE S

All feedback welcomed! If you enjoyed this book we would love to hear from you, and likewise if you have any recommendations for improvement, email us at churchstreetbooks@gmail.com

CONTENTS

CHRISTMAS HYMNS A-Z

1 ANGELS WE HAVE HEARD ON A HIGH

Angels we have heard on high
Sweetly singing o'er the plains
And the mountains in reply
Echoing their joyous strains

Angels we have heard on high
Sweetly, sweetly through the night
And the mountains in reply
Echoing their brief delight

Gloria, in excelsis Deo
Gloria, in excelsis Deo

Shepherds, why this jubilee?
Why your joyous strains prolong?
What the gladsome tidings be
Which inspire your heavenly song?

Gloria, in excelsis Deo
Gloria, in excelsis Deo

Come to Bethlehem and see
Him whose birth the angels sing,
Come, adore on bended knee,
Christ the Lord, the newborn King.

Gloria, in excelsis Deo
Gloria, in excelsis Deo

Yeah
Gloria, in excelsis Deo

Angels we have heard
Angels we have heard on high
Angels we have heard, oh
Angels we have heard on high
Angels we have heard on high
Angels we have heard on high

In excelsis Deo

2 AULD LANG SYNE

Should auld acquaintance be forgot,
and never brought to mind?
Should auld acquaintance be forgot,
and auld lang syne?

For auld lang syne, my jo,
for auld lang syne,
we'll tak a cup o' kindness yet,
for auld lang syne.
And surely ye'll be your pint-stowp!
and surely I'll be mine!
And we'll tak a cup o' kindness yet,
for auld lang syne.

We twa hae run about the braes,
and pu'd the gowans fine;
But we've wander'd mony a weary foot,
sin auld lang syne.

We twa hae paidl'd i' the burn,
frae morning sun till dine;
But seas between us braid hae roar'd
sin auld lang syne.

And there's a hand, my trusty fiere!
and gie's a hand o' thine!
And we'll tak a right gude-willy waught,
for auld lang syne.

For auld lang syne, my jo,
for auld lang syne,
we'll tak a cup o' kindness yet,
for auld lang syne.
And surely ye'll be your pint-stowp!
and surely I'll be mine!
And we'll tak a cup o' kindness yet,
for auld lang syne.

3 AWAY IN THE MANGER

Away in a manger
No crib for His bed
The little Lord Jesus
Lay down His sweet head

The stars in the sky
Look down where He lay
The little Lord Jesus
Asleep on the hay

The cattle are lowing
The poor Baby wakes
But little Lord Jesus
No crying He makes

I love Thee, Lord Jesus
Look down from the sky
And stay by my side
'Til morning is nigh

Be near me, Lord Jesus
I ask Thee to stay
Close by me forever
And love me, I pray

Bless all the dear children
In Thy tender care
And take us to Heaven
To live with Thee there

4 DECK THE HALLS

Deck the halls with boughs of holly
Fa-la-la-la-la, la-la-la-la
'Tis the season to be jolly
Fa-la-la-la-la, la-la-la-la
Don we now our gay apparel
Fa-la-la, la-la-la, la-la-la
Troll the ancient Yule-tide carol
Fa-la-la-la-la, la-la-la-la

Fa-la-la-la-la, la-la-la-la
Fa-la-la-la-la, la-la-la-la
Fa-la-la, la-la-la, la-la-la
Fa-la-la-la-la, la-la-la-la

See the blazing Yule before us
Fa-la-la-la-la, la-la-la-la
Strike the harp and join the chorus
Fa-la-la-la-la, la-la-la-la
Follow me in merry measure
Fa-la-la, la-la-la, la-la-la
While I tell of Yule-tide treasure
Fa-la-la-la-la, la-la-la-la

Fa-la-la-la-la, la-la-la-la

5 DING DONG MERRILY ON HIGH

Ding dong merrily on high,
In heav'n the bells are ringing:
Ding dong! verily the sky
Is riv'n with angel singing
Gloria Hosanna in excelsis!
Gloria Hosanna in excelsis!

E'en so here below, below,
Let steeple bells be swungen,
And "Io, io, io!"
By priest and people sungen
Gloria Hosanna in excelsis!
Gloria Hosanna in excelsis!

Pray you, dutifully prime
Your matin chime, ye ringers,
May you beautifully rhyme
Your eve'time song, ye singers
Gloria Hosanna in excelsis!
Gloria Hosanna in excelsis!

Gloria Hosanna in excelsis!
Gloria Hosanna in excelsis!

Hosanna in excelsis!!!

6 GO TELL IT ON THE MOUNTAINS

Go tell it on the mountain
Over the hills and everywhere
Go tell it on the mountain
Our Jesus Christ is born

When I was a seeker
I sought both night and day
I asked the Lord to help me
And he showed me the way

Go tell it on the mountain
Over the hills and everywhere
Go tell it on the mountain
Our Jesus Christ is born

He made me a watchman
Upon a city wall
And if I am a Christian
I am the least of all

Go tell it on the mountain
Over the hills and everywhere
Go tell it on the mountain
Our Jesus Christ is born

7 GOD REST YE MERRY GENTLEMEN

God rest ye merry gentlemen
Let nothing you dismay
Remember Christ our Savior
Was born on Christmas Day
To save us all from Satan's pow'r
When we were gone astray
Oh tidings of comfort and joy
Comfort and joy
Oh tidings of comfort and joy

God rest ye merry gentlemen
Let nothing you dismay
Remember Christ our Savior
Was born on Christmas Day
To save us all from Satan's pow'r
When we were gone astray
Oh tidings of comfort and joy
Comfort and joy
Oh tidings of comfort and joy

In Bethlehem, in Israel
This blessed Babe was born
And laid within a manger
Upon this blessed morn
The which His Mother Mary
Did nothing take in scorn
Oh tidings of comfort and joy
Comfort and joy
Oh tidings of comfort and joy

Fear not then, said the Angel
Let nothing you affright
This day is born a Savior
Of a pure Virgin bright
To free all those who trust in Him
From Satan's pow'r and might
Oh tidings of comfort and joy
Comfort and joy
Oh tidings of comfort and joy

God rest ye merry gentlemen
Let nothing you dismay
Remember Christ our Savior
Was born on Christmas Day
To save us all from Satan's pow'r
When we were gone astray
Oh tidings of comfort and joy
Comfort and joy
Oh tidings of comfort and joy

8 HARK THE HERALD ANGELS SING

Hark! the herald angels sing,
"Glory to the new-born King!
Peace on earth, and mercy mild,
God and sinners reconciled."
Joyful, all ye nations, rise,
Join the triumph of the skies;
With th' angelic host proclaim,
"Christ is born in Bethlehem."
Hark! the herald angels sing,
"Glory to the new-born King!

Christ, by highest heaven adored:
Christ, the everlasting Lord;
Late in time behold him come,
Offspring of the favoured one.
Veiled in flesh, the Godhead see;
Hail, th'incarnate Deity:
Pleased, as man, with men to dwell,
Jesus, our Emmanuel!
Hark! the herald angels sing,
"Glory to the new-born King!

Hail! the heaven-born
Prince of peace!
Hail! the Son of Righteousness!
Light and life to all he brings,
Risen with healing in his wings
Mild he lays his glory by,
Born that man no more may die:
Born to raise the son of earth,
Born to give them second birth.
Hark! the herald angels sing,
"Glory to the new-born King !"

9 I HEARD THE BELLS ON CHRISTMAS DAY

I heard the bells on Christmas day
Their old familiar carols play
And mild and sweet their songs repeat
Of peace on earth good will to men

And the bells are ringing (peace on earth)
Like a choir they're singing (peace on earth)
In my heart I hear them (peace on earth)
Peace on earth, good will to men

And in despair I bowed my head
There is no peace on earth I said
For hate is strong and mocks the song
Of peace on earth, good will to men

But the bells are ringing (peace on earth)
Like a choir singing (peace on earth)
Does anybody hear them? (peace on earth)
Peace on earth, good will to men

Then rang the bells more loud and deep
God is not dead, nor does he sleep (peace on earth, peace on earth)
The wrong shall fail, the right prevail
With peace on earth, good will to men

Then ringing singing on its way

The world revolved from night to day
A voice, a chime, a chant sublime
Of peace on earth, good will to men

And the bells they're ringing (peace on earth)
Like a choir they're singing (peace on earth)
And with our hearts we'll hear them (peace on earth)
Peace on earth, good will to men

Do you hear the bells they're ringing? (peace on earth)
The life the angels singing (peace on earth)
Open up your heart and hear them (peace on earth)
Peace on earth, good will to men

Peace on earth, peace on earth
Peace on earth, Good will to men

10 I SAW THREE SHIPS

I saw three ships come sailing in
On Christmas Day, on Christmas Day
I saw three ships come sailing in
On Christmas Day in the morning

Wither sailed those ships all three
On Christmas Day, on Christmas Day
Wither sailed those ships all three
On Christmas Day in the morning

Oh they sailed into Bethlehem
On Christmas Day, on Christmas Day
They sailed into Bethlehem
On Christmas Day in the morning

And all the bells on earth shall ring
On Christmas Day, on Christmas Day
And all the bells on earth shall ring
On Christmas Day in the morning

And all the souls on earth shall sing
On Christmas Day, on Christmas Day
And all the souls on earth shall sing
On Christmas Day in the morning

Then let us all rejoice again
On Christmas Day, on Christmas Day
Then let us all rejoice again
On Christmas Day in the morning

I saw three ships come sailing in
On Christmas Day, on Christmas Day
I saw three ships come sailing in
On Christmas Day in the morning

I saw three ships come sailing in
On Christmas Day, on Christmas Day
I saw three ships come sailing in
On Christmas Day in the morning

11 IT CAME UPON A MIDNIGHT CLEAR

It came upon the midnight clear
That glorious song of old
From Angels playing near the earth
To touch their harps of gold

Peace on the earth could will two men
From Heaven's all-gracious King
The world in solemn stillness lay
To hear the Angels sing

And I hear them singing
Sing, I do hear them singing

The first Noel the Angel did say
Was to certain poor shepherds in fields as they lay
In fields where they lay, they keeping their sheep
On a cold winter's night that was so deep

12 JINGLE BELLS

Jingle bells, jingle bells
Jingle all the way,
Oh what fun it is to ride
In a one-horse open sleigh,
Jingle bells, jingle bells
Jingle all the way,
Oh what fun it is to ride
In a one-horse open sleigh.

Dashing through the snow
In a one-horse open sleigh
Through the fields we go
Laughing all the way.
Bells on bob-tail ring
Making spirits bright
What fun it is to ride and sing
A sleighing song tonight.

Jingle bells, jing-jingle bells
Jingle all the way,
Oh what fun it is to ride
In a one-horse open sleigh, brruup
Jingle bells, jingle bells
Jingle all the way,
Oh what fun it is to ride
In a one-horse open sleigh.

Dashing through the snow
In a one-horse open sleigh
Through the fields we go
Laughing all the way.
Bells on bob-tail ring
Making spirits bright
What fun it is to ride and sing
A sleighing song tonight.

Jingle bells, jingle bells
Jingle all the way,
Oh what fun it is to ride
In a one-horse open sleigh,
Jingle bells, jingle bells
Jingle all the way,
Oh what fun it is to ride
In a one-horse open sleigh.

Jingle bells, jingle bells
Jingle all the way,
Oh what fun it is to ride
In a one-horse open sleigh,
Jingle bells, jingle bells
Jingle all the way,
Oh what fun it is to ride
In a one-horse open sleigh.

13 JOY TO THE WORLD

Joy to the world
Joy to the world
Joy to the world, the Lord is come
Let earth receive her King
Let every heart prepare Him room
And Heaven and nature sing
And Heaven and nature sing
And Heaven, and Heaven, and nature sing

Joy to the world
Joy to the world
Joy to the World, the Savior reigns!
Let men their songs employ
While fields and floods, rocks, hills and plains
Repeat the sounding joy
Repeat the sounding joy
Repeat, repeat, the sounding joy

Joy to the world, now we sing
Let the earth receive her king
Joy to the world, now we sing
Let the angel voices ring
Joy to the world, now we sing
Let men their songs employ
Joy to the world, now we sing
Repeat the sounding joy

Oh oh
He rules the world with truth and grace
And makes the nations prove
The light of His righteousness
And wonders of His love
And wonders of His love
And wonders of His love
And wonders, wonders, of His love
And wonders, wonders, of His love

Joy to the world, now we sing
Let the earth receive her king
Joy to the world, now we sing
Let the angel voices ring

14 LITTLE DONKEY

Little donkey, little donkey on the dusty road
Got to keep on plodding onwards with your precious load
Been a long time, little donkey, through the winters night
don't give up now, little donkey,
Bethlehems in sight

Ring out those bells tonight
Bethlehem, Bethlehem
Follow that star tonight
Bethlehem, Bethlehem

Little donkey, little donkey, had a heavy day
Little donkey, carry Mary safely on her way
Little donkey, little donkey, journey's end is near
There are wiseman waiting for a sign to bring them here

Do not falter little donkey, there's a star ahead
It will guide you, little donkey, to a cattle shed

Ring out those bells tonight
Bethlehem, Bethlehem
Follow that star tonight
Bethlehem, Bethlehem

Little donkey, little donkey, had a heavy day
Little donkey, carry Mary, safely on her way
Little donkey, carry Mary, safely on her way

15 O COME, ALL YE FAITHFUL

O come, all ye faithful
Joyful and triumphant
O come ye, o come ye to Bethlehem
Come and behold Him
Born the King of Angels!

O come, let us adore Him
O come, let us adore Him
O come, let us adore Him
Christ the Lord

O come, all ye faithful
O come, all ye faithful
O come, all ye faithful to Bethlehem
O come, all ye faithful
O come, all ye faithful
O come, all ye faithful to Bethlehem

Oh, sing, choirs of angels
Sing in exultation
Oh, come, oh come ye to Bethlehem
Come and behold Him
Born the King of Angels

O come, let us adore Him
O come, let us adore Him
O come, let us adore Him
Christ the Lord

O come, all ye faithful
O come, all ye faithful
O come, all ye faithful to Bethlehem
O come, all ye faithful
O come, all ye faithful
O come, all ye faithful to Bethlehem

O come, all ye
O come, all ye faithful
O come, all ye
O come, all ye faithful
O come, all ye
O come, all ye faithful
O come, all ye
O come, all ye faithful
O come, all ye
O come, all ye faithful
O come, all ye
O come, all ye faithful
O come, all ye
O come, all ye faithful
O come, all ye
O come, all ye faithful

O come, all ye faithful
O come, all ye faithful
O come, all ye faithful to Bethlehem

O come, all ye faithful
(O come, all ye faithful, o come, all ye faithful)
Joyful and triumphant
(O come, all ye faithful to Bethlehem)
Come and behold Him
(O come, all ye faithful, o come, all ye faithful)
Born the King of Angels

O come, let us adore Him
O come, let us adore Him
O come, let us adore Him
Christ the Lord

O come, all ye faithful
O come, all ye faithful
O come, all ye faithful to Bethlehem

16 O HOLY NIGHT

O holy night the stars are brightly shining
It is the night of our dear Savior's birth
Long lay the world in sin and error pining
Till He appeared and the soul felt its worth

A thrill of hope the weary world rejoices
For yonder breaks a new glorious morn
Fall on your knees
O hear the angels' voices
O night divine
O night when Christ was born
O night divine o night
O night divine

A thrill of hope the weary world rejoices
For yonder breaks a new glorious morn
Fall on your knees
O hear the angels' voices

O night divine
O night when Christ was born
O night divine o night
O night divine
Ooh yes it was
Ooh it is the night of our dear Savior's birth
Oh yeah, oh yeah, oh yeah, yeah
It was a holy holy holy, oh oh oh

17 O LITTLE TOWN OF BETHLEHEM

O little town of Bethlehem
How still we see thee lie
Above thy deep and dreamless sleep
The silent stars go by
Yet in thy dark streets shineth
The everlasting Light
The hopes and fears of all the years
Are met in thee tonight

For Christ is born of Mary
And gathered all above
While mortals sleep, the angels keep
Their watch of wondering love
O morning stars together
Proclaim the holy birth
And praises sing to God the King
And Peace to men on earth

Away in a manger
No crib for a bed
The little Lord Jesus
Lay down His sweet head
The stars in the sky
Look down where He lay
The little Lord Jesus
Asleep on the hay
Asleep on the hay

O holy Child of Bethlehem
Descend to us, we pray
Cast out our sin and enter in
Be born to us today
We hear the Christmas angels
The great glad tidings tell
O come to us, abide with us
Our Lord Emmanuel

18 ONCE IN ROYAL DAVID'S CITY

Once in royal David's city,
Stood a lowly cattle shed,
Where a mother laid her baby
In a manger for His bed:
Mary was that mother mild,
Jesus Christ her little child.

He came down to earth from heaven,
Who is God and Lord of all,
And His shelter was a stable,
And His cradle was a stall;
With the poor and meek and lowly,
Lived on earth our Savior holy.

And through all
His wondrous childhood,
He would honor and obey,
Love and watch the lowly mother,
In whose gentle arms He lay.
Christian children all should be,
Mild, obedient, good as He.

For He is our child-hood's pattern,
Day by day like us He grew,
He was little, weak, and helpless,
Tears and smiles like us He knew,
And He feeleth for our sadness,
And He shareth in our gladness.

And our eyes at last shall see Him,
Through His own redeeming love;
For that child so dear and gentle,
Is our Lord in heaven above,
And He leads His children on,
To the place where He is gone.

Not in that poor lowly stable,
With the oxen standing by,
We shall see Him, but in heaven,
Set at God's right hand on high;
When like stars
His children crowned,
All in white shall be around.

19 SILENT NIGHT

Silent night, holy night
All is calm, all is bright
Round yon Virgin, Mother, Mother and Child
Holy infant so tender and mild
Sleep in heavenly peace
Sleep in heavenly

Sleep in heavenly
Sleep in heavenly
Sleep in heavenly
Sleep in heavenly peace

Silent night, holy night
All is calm, all is bright
Round yon Virgin, Mother, Mother and Child
Holy infant so tender and mild
Sleep in heavenly peace
Sleep in heavenly peace

Christ, Christ, the Savior is born
Christ, Christ, the Savior
Christ, Christ, the Savior is born

20 STAR OF THE EAST

Star of the East, Oh Bethlehem's star,
Guiding us on to Heaven afar!
Sorrow and grief and lull'd by thy light,
Thou hope of each mortal, in death's lonely night!

Fearless and tranquil, we look up to Thee!
Knowing thou beam'st thro' eternity!
Help us to follow where Thou still dost guide,
Pilgrims of earth so wide.

Star of the East, thou hope of the soul,
While round us here the dark billows roll,
Lead us from sin to glory afar,
Thou star of the East, thou sweet Bethlehem's star.

Star of the East, un-dim'd by each cloud,
What tho' the storms of grief gather loud?
Faithful and pure thy rays beam to save,
Still bright o'er the cradle, and bright o'er the grave!

Smiles of a Saviour are mirror'd in Thee!
Glimpses of Heav'n in thy light we see!
Guide us still onward to that blessed shore,
After earth's toil is o'er!

Star of the East, thou hope of the soul,
While round us here the dark billows roll,
Lead us from sin to glory afar,
Thou star of the East, thou sweet Bethlehem's star.

Oh star that leads to God above!
Whose rays are peace and joy and love!
Watch o'er us still till life hath ceased,
Beam on, bright star, sweet Bethlehem star!

21 THE FIRST NOEL

Noel, Noel
Noel, Noel
The First Noel, the Angels did say
Was to certain poor shepherds in fields as they lay
In fields where they lay keeping their sheep
On a cold winter's night that was so deep
Noel, Noel, Noel, Noel
Born is the King of Israel!
Noel, Noel
Noel, Noel

They looked up and saw a star
Shining in the East beyond them far
And to the earth it gave great light
And so it continued both day and night
Noel, Noel
Noel, Noel
Noel, Noel
Noel, Noel
Noel, Noel
Noel, Noel
Born is the King of Israel!

Noel, Noel, Noel, Noel
Born is the King of Israel!
Born is the King of Israel!
Noel, Noel
Noel, Noel

22 THERE'S A SONG IN THE AIR

There's a song in the air! There's a star in the sky!
There's a mother's deep prayer and a baby's low cry!
And the star rains its fire while the beautiful sing,
For the manger of Bethlehem cradles a King!

There's a tumult of joy o'er the wonderful birth,
For the virgin's sweet Boy is the Lord of the earth.
Ay! the star rains its fire while the beautiful sing,
For the manger of Bethlehem cradles a King!

In the light of that star lie the ages impearled;
And that song from afar has swept over the world.
Every hearth is aflame, and the beautiful sing
In the homes of the nations that Jesus is King!

We rejoice in the light, and we echo the song
That comes down through the night from the heavenly throng.
Ay! we shout to the lovely evangel they bring,
And we greet in His cradle our Savior and King!

23 TOYLAND

Toyland, toyland
Little girl and boy land
While you dwell within it
You are ever happy there

Childhood's joy land
Mystic merry toyland
Once you pass its borders
You can ne'er return again

When you've grown up, my dears
And are as old as I
You'll laugh and ponder on the years
That roll so swiftly by, my dears
That roll so swiftly by

Childhood's joy land
Mystic merry toyland
Once you pass its borders
You can ne'er return again

24 THE TWELVE DAYS OF CHRISTMAS

On the first day of Christmas my true love sent to me
A partridge in a pear tree

On the second day of Christmas my true love sent to me
Two turtle doves
And a partridge in a pear tree

On the third day of Christmas my true love sent to me
Three French hens, two turtle doves
And a partridge in a pear tree

On the fourth day of Christmas my true love sent to me
Four calling birds, three French hens, two turtle doves
And a partridge in a pear tree

On the fifth day of Christmas my true love sent to me
Five gold rings, four calling birds, three French hens, two
turtle doves
And a partridge in a pear tree

On the sixth day of Christmas my true love sent to me
Six geese a laying, five gold rings, four calling birds
Three French hens, two turtle doves
And a partridge in a pear tree

On the seventh day of Christmas my true love sent to me
Seven swans a swimming, six geese a laying, five gold rings
Four calling birds, three French hens, two turtle doves
And a partridge in a pear tree

On the eighth day of Christmas my true love sent to me
Eight maids a milking, seven swans a swimming, six geese a
laying
Five gold rings, four calling birds, three French hens, two
turtle doves
And a partridge in a pear tree

On the ninth day of Christmas my true love sent to me
Nine drummers drumming, eight maids a milking, seven
swans a swimming, six geese a laying
Five gold rings, four calling birds, three French hens, two
turtle doves
And a partridge in a pear tree

On the tenth day of Christmas my true love sent to me
Ten pipers piping
Nine drummers drumming, eight maids a milking, seven
swans a swimming, six geese a laying
Five gold rings, four calling birds, three French hens, two
turtle doves
And a partridge in a pear tree

On the eleventh day of Christmas my true love sent to me
Eleven ladies dancing, ten pipers piping, nine drummers
drumming
Eight maids a milking, seven swans a swimming, six geese a
laying
Five gold rings, four calling birds, three French hens, two
turtle doves
And a partridge in a pear tree

On the twelfth day of Christmas my true love sent to me
Twelve Lords a leaping, eleven ladies dancing, ten pipers
piping
Nine, drummers drumming, eight maids a milking
Seven swans a swimming, six geese a laying
And five gold rings, four calling birds, three French hens,
two turtle doves
And a partridge in a pear tree, and a partridge in a pear
tree

25 UP ON THE HOUSETOP

Up on the housetop, reindeer pause
Out jumps good ol' Santa Claus
Down through the chimney with lots of toys
All for the little ones, Christmas joys
Ho, Ho, Ho! Who wouldn't go?
Ho, Ho, Ho! Who wouldn't go?
Up on the housetop, click, click, click
Down through the chimney with good Saint Nick

First comes the stocking of little Nell
Oh, dear Santa, fill it well
Give her a dolly that laughs and cries
One that will open and shut her eyes
Ho, Ho, Ho! Who wouldn't go?
Ho, Ho, Ho! Who wouldn't go?
Up on the housetop, click, click, click
Down through the chimney with good Saint Nick

Next comes the stocking of little Will
Oh, just see what a glorious fill
Here is a hammer and lots of tacks
Also a ball and a whip that cracks
Ho, Ho, Ho! Who wouldn't go?
Ho, Ho, Ho! Who wouldn't go?
Up on the housetop, click, click, click
Down through the chimney with good Saint Nick
What'd ya-know? its 'ol Saint Nick!

26 WE THREE KINGS

We three kings of orient are,
Bearing gifts we traverse afar
Field and fountain, moor and mountain,
Following yonder star.

Oh, star of wonder, star of night,
Star with royal beauty bright.
Westward leading, still proceeding,
Guide with thy perfect light.

Born a King on Bethlehem's plain,
Gold I bring to crown him again
King for ever, ceasing never
Over us all to reign.

Frankincense to offer have I, incense owns a Deity nigh
Pray'r and praising, all men raising,
Worship him, God most high, oh

27 WE WISH YOU A MERRY CHRISTMAS

We wish you a Merry Christmas
We wish you a Merry Christmas
We wish you a Merry Christmas and a Happy New Year!
Good tidings we bring to you and your kin
We wish you a Merry Christmas and a Happy New Year!
We all want some figgy pudding
We all want some figgy pudding
We all want some figgy pudding, so bring some right here.
We won't go until we get some
We won't go until we get some
We won't go until we get some, so bring some right here.
Good tidings we bring to you and your kin
We wish you a Merry Christmas and a Happy New Year.
Good tidings we bring to you and your kin
We wish you a Merry Christmas and a Happy New Year!
We wish you a Merry Christmas
We wish you a Merry Christmas
We wish you a Merry Christmas and a Happy New Year!
We wish you a Merry Christmas
We wish you a Merry Christmas
We wish you a Merry Christmas and a Happy New Year!

28 WHAT CHILD IS THIS?

What Child is this
Who laid to rest
On Mary's lap is sleeping?
Whom Angels greet with anthems sweet,
While shepherds watch are keeping?

So bring Him incense, gold and myrrh,
Come Peasant, King to own Him
The King of Kings salvation brings,
Let loving hearts enthrone Him.

This, this is Christ the King,
Whom shepherds guard and Angels sing
Haste, haste, to bring Him laud,
The Babe, the Son of Mary.

Oh, raise, raise a song on high,
His mother sings her lullaby.
Joy, oh joy for Christ is born,
The Babe, the Son of Mary.

This, this is Christ the King,
Whom shepherds guard and Angels sing

Haste, haste, to bring Him laud,
The Babe,
The Son,
Of Mary.

What Child
Is this
Who laid
To rest
On Mary's lap
On Mary's lap
He is sleeping

This, this is Christ the King,
Whom shepherds guard and Angels sing
Haste, haste, to bring Him laud,
The Babe,
The Son,
Of Mary

The Babe, the Son of Mary

The Son of Mary

Printed in Great Britain
by Amazon